Relax
FOR THE
Fun
OF IT

By Allan Hirsh, M.A.

Caramal Publishing Inc.
P.O. Box 29022,
Vancouver, BC, V6J 5C2, Canada
www.caramal.com

National Library of Canada Cataloguing in Publication Data
Hirsh, Allan, 1948-
Relax for the fun of it [kit] : a cartoon & audio guide to releasing stress
Includes bibliographical references.
ISBN 0-9685421-1-5
1. Stress management — Caricatures and cartoons.
2. Canadian wit and humor, Pictorial. I. Title
BF575.S75H57 2002   741.5'971   C2001-901373-6

Printed in Canada
First Edition

Cover Design by Mariana Prins
Book Design by Mariana Prins
Illustrations by Allan Hirsh

CARAMAL PUBLISHING

To my parents,
Rose and Sydney Hirsh,
for their love, humor and
belief in me.

PUBLISHER'S NOTE

The purpose of this book is educate and entertain.
This book serves as a humorous introduction to
stress management and is not a substitute for
psychotherapy or other suitable professional help.
Please do not listen to the Relaxation CD while
operating a vehicle.

ACKNOWLEDGEMENTS

SPECIAL THANKS TO:

LYNN JOHNSTON
ALAN RAPKIN
JOAN FERNEYHOUGH
JACOB AND JOSHUA HIRSH
ELISSA ODGREN
BARRY SPILCHUK

INTRODUCTION

If we can laugh at our problems, we'll always have something to laugh about. Loving, gentle humor helps us feel lighter and more relaxed. Humor opens the doors that stress, tension and pain have closed. Humor can also help channel stress into something productive. Laughter can provide a distance from pain, which helps us to keep matters in perspective.

Humor alone, however, will not cure baldness or solve all problems. It's important not to get too tired, hungry, or negative. If we do, coping becomes difficult and we're more likely to overreact and make ourselves even more miserable. Humor and a snack help with the negativity and hunger, but sometimes our bodies just need to rest and unwind.

In the back of this book is a sixteen minute relaxation CD. It is straightforward and effective. The CD has two tracks on it. The first track is sixteen minutes long and includes a gentle wake-up, so that you can continue with your day, refreshed and alert. The second track does not have a wake up so you can drift off into a pleasant sleep, if you so choose. By following the instructions on the CD, you will gradually become more aware of the muscles of your body, and your ability to release tension. In a short period of time, you will find yourself automatically relaxing parts of your body without even giving it much thought. When I was a student, I had a tension headache every day. My neck muscles would tighten up during the course of the day, and I had no idea what to do about it. I wish I had learned to relax earlier in my life.

You may want to follow the instructions on the CD first, or, start by reading the humorous guide on relaxation and stress management instead. It really doesn't matter. Learning to cope with stress is often a trial and error process. Sometimes you'll find that laughter will lighten your mood best. At other times, a few moments of physical relaxation will be your ticket back to comfort.

Relaxation is not a discipline, nor is it a chore. Your body looks forward to the pleasure and relief of unwinding. Relaxing is as natural to the body as laughing. All we need to do is open ourselves to the feeling; it's as effortless as a cat beginning to purr. The technique is not as important as the end result of relaxation.

Do what works for you. Do what you feel is fun. If you like the experience, you will naturally do it again. I love to relax. I take 16 minutes out of every day to take a mini-vacation.

May the joy of living gently tap you on your shoulder when you least expect it.

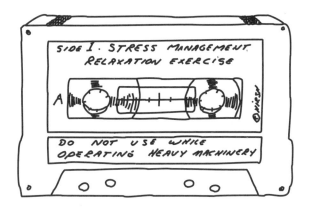

ALSO AVAILABLE IN 8-TRACK AND BETA

A **relaxed body** is a **wonderful** sensation. Please don't try too hard when practising the art of relaxation.

First become **aware** of your muscles by **tensing** them...

...and then **relax** your **muscles.**

Notice the differences between the sensations of tension and the sensations of relaxation.

NOT RELAXED   RELAXED

Just **thinking** of the body **relaxing** allows tension to leave.

The more you use the relaxation CD, the easier it will be to relax.

You will gradually become able to relax your muscles whenever you wish.

PRACTISE RELAXATION WHEN
YOU ARE HAVING A HARD DAY

AND FINDING IT DIFFICULT TO GO WITH THE FLOW

Try to **do something** about your tension **before** you **feel** overwhelmed.

Running into
a few
frustrations
during the day?

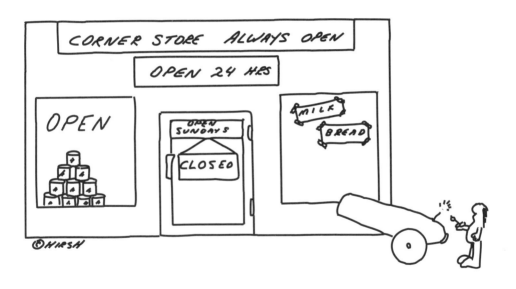

Anticipating the worst?

Relaxation

helps when...

Unfortunately,
stress is

part of everyday
life.

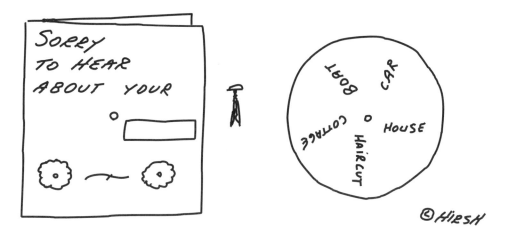

Sometimes
it **helps**
to
shift gears
and **slow
down**.

"Sleep faster !
We **need** the
pillows."

- an old Jewish expression

Unwind
for
a few
moments.

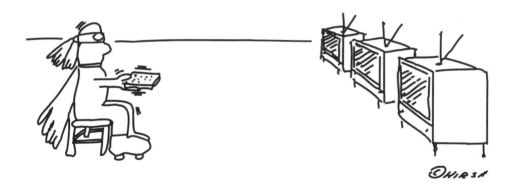

"TYPE-A MAN" IN A RARE MOMENT OF T.V. WATCHING

Take the **time** to **connect** with **someone**.

"TYPE-A MAN" HAS A HEART TO HEART TALK WITH HIS WIFE

You can tune in and out of different **levels** of **awareness** all the time.

You can tune away from your worries for a few moments and become more aware of the smell of a flower, the smile of a child, or the relaxing sensations of a deep breath.

Pace yourself and avoid **burnout**.

Pace yourself and avoid **arguments**.

A **touch** of **relaxation** can bring people **closer**...

Sometimes **simple experiences** can foster relaxation. With **gentle** curiosity, witness your inner **reaction** to a few moments of **creativity:** Imagine the perfect bath...

What incredible **features** would you include?

Did you include a sound system, lighting control, and a contoured head rest?

Without creativity our **responses** to situations become **rigid.**

Clasp your hands...
which thumb is on top?

Now switch your hands so that
the other thumb is on top.

Even little **changes** in life
seem **uncomfortable**
at times.

What is this?

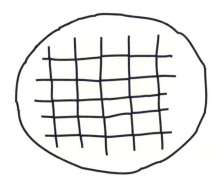

1. Peanut butter **cookie**?

2. Top **view** of an obsessive compulsive balding man?

Creativity and **humor** can help shift your mind into a **lighter** mode.

What
totally
absorbed
you as a
child?

What
was your
favourite
activity?

What do you
need to **do** to **feel**
better
about **yourself?**

Gardening can **nurture** the **soul**...

Your **body** often has profound wisdom, **listen** to the message. Then **do** something **positive** for your body.

Regular **exercise** helps to **release** frustration, manage stress, and **strengthen** your body.

Go at your own pace and you'll begin to **enjoy** yourself.

Yoga postures can help **stretch** and **relax** your body... begin **gently**.

1957 HOOD ORNAMENT POSE

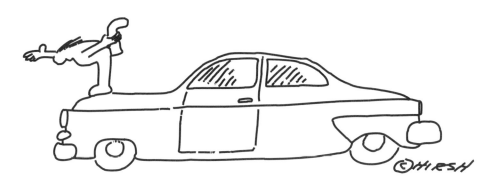

Choose a **pleasant** pastime...

Meditation involves
focusing
your **mind** on your
breath, a prayer,
an image, or
a calming sound.

Healthy food
is as **good** for your body
as a joyous laugh.

Sometimes you can
feel good about yourself
by reaching for a **goal**.

Sometimes you can
enjoy 'the doing' and
lose yourself in the **moment**.

Sometimes you can
simply be.

Imagine yourself in **comfort** and make a **wish**.

If all else fails,
perhaps **professional**
help would be useful.
Choose a **therapist** you
feel **comfortable**
with.

Find a **quiet** moment
and **look** within.

Nourish your body
with health and relaxation,
shift your **mind**
with creativity and humor,
warm your heart through
play and **love.**

Attend lectures
that help
expand your
awareness.

Why not take
a few **moments**
to relax?

Your **relaxation**
CD is only sixteen
minutes long.

Please do the relaxation in a way that feels **comfortable** to you.

Choose a **time**, place and position that suits your needs.

Experiment. Enjoy.

If you have back problems, you may want to lie on your back with pillows under your knees. Relax the body and the mind will eventually follow.

I wish you peace and joy.

RELAXATION

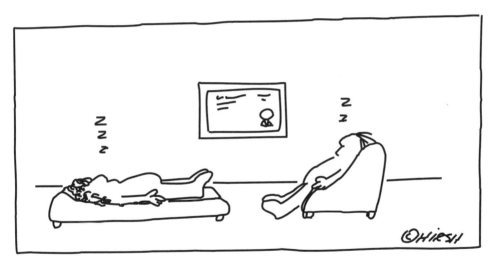

BIBLIOGRAPHY

Axline, Virginia Dibs. *In Search of Self*. New York: Ballentine, 1964.

Black, Claudia. *It's Never Too Late To Have A Happy Childhood*.
New York: Ballantine, 1989.

Bloom, Lynn and Coburn, Karen and Pearlman, Joan. *The New Assertive Woman*.
New York: Delacorte Press, 1975.

Bradshaw, John. *Homecoming*. New York: Bantam, 1990.

Delaney, Gayle. *All About Dreams*. San Francisco: Harper, 1998.

Fischer, Ed and Haebig, Jeff. *Toon Ups, Self-Health Humor*.
Rochester: Wellness Quest, 1995.

Ford, Judy. *Getting Over Getting Mad*. Berkely: Conari Press, 2001.

Frankl, Victor. *Man's Search for Meaning*. New York: Touchstone, 1984.

Gendlin, Eugene. *Focusing*. New York: Bantam, 1981.

Hesse, Hermann. *Siddhartha* (translated by Hilda Rosner). London: Owen, 1964.

Jeffers, Susan. *Feel the Fear and Do It Anyway*. New York: Fawcett Columbine, 1987.

Johanson, Greg and Kurtz, Ron. *Psychotherapy in the Spirit of Tao-te ching*.
New York: Bell Tower, 1991.

Lazarus, Arnold. *I Can If I Want To*. New York: Warner Books, 1977.

Lerner, Harriet. *The Dance of Anger*. New York: Harper and Row, 1985.

Lerner, Rokelle. *Affirmations for the Inner Child*. Deerfield Beach, Health
Communications, 1990.

Louden, Jennifer. *The Woman's Comfort Book*. San Francisco: Harper, 1992.

Maratta and Maratta. *Counter Culture (cartoons)*. New York: Topper Books, 1989.

Mc-Gee-Cooper, Anne. *You Don't Have To Come Home From Work Exhausted!*
New York: Bantam, 1992.

Meddick, Jim. *Primary Crullers, A Robotman Book (cartoons)*.
Kansas City: Andrews Mc Meel, 1997.

O'Brian, Richard. *The Story of American Toys*. New York: Abbeville Press, 1990.

Persig, Robert. *Zen and the Art of Motorcycle Maintenance*. New York: Bantam, 1974.

Richardson, Frank and Woolfolk, Robert. *Stress, Sanity, & Survival*.
New York: Signet, 1979.

Rinker Jr., Harry. *Flea Market Treasures*. Radnor: Wallace-Homestead Books, 1995.

Samuels, Mike and Samuels, Nancy. *Seeing With the Mind's Eye*.
New York: Random House, 1975.

Satir, Virginia. *Peoplemaking*. Palo Alto: Science and Behavior Books, 1972.

Siegel, Bernie. *Peace, Love and Healing*. New York: Harper and Row, 1989.

Smith, Manuel. *When I say No, I Feel Guilty*. New York: Bantam, 1975.

Time Life Books. *Complete Fix-It-Yourself Manual*. New York: Prentice Hall, 1989.

Welch, David and Medeiros, Donald and Tate, George. *Beyond Burnout*.
New Jersey: Prentice-Hall, 1982

White, John and Fadiman, James. *Relax*. Confucian Press, 1976.

Allan Hirsh, M.A.
Counselling Services
348 Fraser, Suite 203
North Bay, Ontario
Canada, P1B 3W7

www.allanhirsh.com
e-mail: relax@allanhirsh.com

ORDER FORM

Order on-line at: http://www.caramal.com

Telephone Orders: Call toll-free 1-888-866-7745 (or 512-288-5005)

Bulk Orders: Call for discount pricing on 5 books or more, or e-mail: service@caramal.com

Fax Orders: Please fill out this form and fax it to: 512-288-5055

Postal Orders: Please fill out this form and mail it to:
Caramal Publishing, PO Box 29022, Vancouver, BC., V6J 5C2, Canada

Please send (   ) copies of Relax For The Fun Of It to:

Name: _____ Address: _____

_____

City & State/Province: _____ Zip/Postal Code: _____

Country: _____ Telephone: (   ) _____

Shipping: USA & Canada: $4 for the first book and $2 for each additional book.
International: $9 for the first book and $4 for each additional book.

Figure Out The Cost:

(   ) copies of Relax For The Fun Of It @ $19.95 each = _____

Texas Residents add 8.25% ($1.65) sales tax = _____

Shipping Charges = _____

Total Payment Due = _____

All prices are in U.S. Dollars

Payment: Cheque (must be in U.S. Dollars)
Money Order / Bank Draft (must be in U.S.Dollars)
Credit Card: ☐Visa ☐Mastercard ☐American Express
Card Number: _____
Name on Card: _____ Expiry date: ___ / _____